THE
SEED
THIEVES

poems by

ROBERT FANNING

MARICK PRESS

Library of Congress Cataloging in Publication Data

Fanning, Robert
The Seed Thieves.
Poems in English
ISBN 0-9779703-0-2

Copyright © Robert Fanning, 2006
Edited by Peter Markus
Design and typesetting by Sean Tai
Cover design by Sean Tai

Cover art: "What Should We Do?" Sculptural installation by
Denise Whitebread Fanning, Tangent Gallery, Detroit, MI.
Cover photograph by Daniel Marlow.
Author photograph by Jerome Burns.

Printed and bound in Canada

Marick Press
P.O. Box 36253
Grosse Pointe Farms
Michigan 48236
www.marickpress.com

Distributed by spdbooks.org

for Denise and Gabriel

For Daniel—
a comrade in this art
Good luck writing,
Robert.
11.4.09
Mt. Pleasant, MI.

Contents

Blueprint of the Ruins   1

I

Light's Bright Lies   5
Failed Existentialist in a Field of Fireflies   6
Dying Star   7
The Leaving   9
Standing in the Shed Light   10
One and a Half Miles Away from Dying   11

II

Interstate 75   15
Skyline Angel   18
Death Revisited   19
Live Worms Found in Shuttle Debris   21
All Heaven's Hotline Switchboard Lights   23
The Messiah Complex   25
One Day I Will Rule the World   27
The Man Who Names Wars   29
Making Sure the Tractor Works   31
Crooked Wisdom   33
Heimlich in Candlelight   35
Boy with a Trumpet in a Burning House   36
Shepherds and Angels   38
Still Shot   39
Scarecrow Cross   42
Morning Glory   43

III

The Discovery of Fire	47
Watching the Wind Read	48
The Perfect Poem	50
Digital Intimates	51
Last Dancers	52
The Pioneers	53
All the Mind's Animals	54
Jellyfish	55
My Old Flame	56

IV

The Cloth Wings of the Woman	59
Seaside Carnival, Late in the World	61
Old Bright Wheel	63
The Roller Coaster	65
Picturing the Lost World	67
Happiness	68
The Slide King	70
The List of Good Names	72
Tributary	74

V

Green Stephania	77
Pedinkis	79
John's Knees	80
Sissy	81
Killer Raccoons at Sleeping Bear Dunes	82
Gullsong August	84
For My Wife, Who Sleeps	85
Song of the Sea to the Shore	87
Song of the Shore to the Sea	88
Acknowledgments	90
Biographical Note	92

By the sea's side hear the dark-vowelled birds.
—Dylan Thomas

Well, I've been praying a lot lately, because I no longer have a TV.
—Mark Eitzel

Blueprint of the Ruins

Here's the front door
    approximately. Here's the threshold,
    the opening

to a room of charred walls.
    Before us now, half-razed beams,
    the intricate architecture

of rubble. In our hands,
    this map of a place once here,
    recovered from ash.

What will we make of this light
    through which, now lifting its beams
    in emptiness, it's clear

how the dust unsettles us,
    and how, even lifting our hands to pray
    we disturb the air.

I

Light's Bright Lies

Tonight I leave the white electric hum
of streetlights, those killing globes that cause
moths their last thrusts of faith and delirium.
Dumb believers, starving for light, the gauze
of their dead wings covers my fingers with dust.
I've learned from them a daring trust

in darkness saves a life. Tonight I leave
the tease of light's bright lies—
that led me, by its touch, to believe
I see. Walking through a dark field, my eyes
give in. Behind their lenses, in absence
of light, another aperture opens—the same sense

with which I watch in every sleep a life
inside my life take shape—as if another light
goes on beneath: a ship's lamp scanning reefs
that reveals a cave once lost to sight.
In that world shines a silver streaking eel,
the real light, that burns by what it feels.

Failed Existentialist in a Field of Fireflies

A blizzard of absurd low stars,

        or searchlights

               on a far shore,

this dance of tiny fires

draws me
in. I watch

      within the larger darkness

           these flares ignite—

    this green flurry
       a bright show
         of force
against a black sea;

they surface, disappear

          and surface again.

     From what flames do these

           rise, these embers
     flashing over me.

How can I,
    who've outlived God, survive

     this sudden desire to pray?

Dying Star

You appear in only one scene, late
in the last act—the curtains part
and there you sit: a bloodied, blue-lipped
lump of a body, slumped center stage.

The lead lady screams over you—her dead
secret lover. Stillborn into the life
of the stage, you disappear after one role—
no spotlight bows, no thrown bouquets,

no afterglow. Curtains closed, houselights up,
your name buried in a program out in the slush.
But for this brief center stage appearance
you spent hours rehearsing every nuance

and gesture: of the man who sits for hours
on the park bench, barely blinking;
of Sunday's congregation, dozing through
homilies; of shopping mall hordes dragging

bags and blank stares; of the local mortician
eyeing a gray slab of meat in the late night
diner. No one noticed as you hunched
like a vulture in the wings, watching, perfecting

the fine art of stopping your heart.
Even in your only scene, lost in the umbra
of the darling starlet, you're invisible as dust
circling the spotlight's long beam. Understudy

of everyone alive, short-lived star, it's *you, Death*,
we'll recognize too late, behind hospital curtains
in passing, as we leave our own small stage—
relinquishing each letter of our famous names to you.

The Leaving

Even the season won't let go.
All bristle and lean in a late tease
of autumn heat, clustered sunflowers
wither and blacken in the field's far fray.
In heaped embers of clouds, thousands of birds

scatter over harvested distances in search
of the past months' dalliance and shine.
A branch of great hearts, the last red leaves
hang from a tree blown bare. They drag in air:
shawled and trailing widows, hunched

forward in the driven wind. Even in this show,
this late flare of life, nothing saves from the tearing
away, from grief's encroaching freeze. Through
the flagrant headstones, a mourning fold rolls
to a fresh grave's edge:

over the deepest of holes, they teeter between here
and gone. If they've loved, if they've tangled roots
with the leaving, this dying rushes through. As they turn
toward the sudden wind shift and chill, in each
the heart's strange flame dims then leaps—
snuffed, then struck twice alive.

Standing in the Shed Light

All day long, the line of sunlight
inches up the grass toward
the open door of the dead

man's darkened shed,
where all the accumulated tools
of a lifetime still hang

from their crooked hooks.
At sunset, I stand
at the shed's bright entrance

staring at the wall,
at the abandoned tools
shining as if lit from within.

A pile of rusted nails
sneers, cowering inside
the shadow thrown by my body.

In my hand now
the heavy hammer
burns and glows.

One and a Half Miles Away from Dying

the people in this car, unaware
their sacred closing moments are here,
exhaust their last travel game.
In the back seat the girl hums,

braiding her sister's black hair.
The boy traces his name in breath
on the back window, each slow letter
squeaking the chilled glass, making his mother

shiver. Like a fish trapped in thin pond
ice, gasping, she stares into the car
through the visor vanity mirror.
Her lips glisten under the lipstick wand.

Yawning, the driver's face is caught wide open
in passing headlight amber, his left hand
draped over the wheel at the wrist.
His other hand tries to retrieve the lost

voice of *The Late World News* reporter,
her words garbled by cloudbursts
shattering over the flat horizon, east.
Shutting the radio off, he tries to lure

his kids to sing one they know by heart.
He turns the rearview mirror until it
holds their three faces. Half in shadow,
placid, they peer at him below,

his cheeks splashed green by dashboard light.
The clock's last digit clicks one more minute.
Beyond the blind curve, a truck's hulk
of silver screeches over the median wall.

An oil tanker, sparks raging, airborne,
careens toward this side of the freeway
—meteor tail of flame, like a missile shot
astray. Back in the car, before the turn,

it is quiet. The people smile
doing last minute things:
one scratching an ankle,
one blinking,
one taking a breath preparing to sing.

II

Interstate 75

This is the season the dark comes soon.
Something dives
through the evening's tar-black sky,
swooping above the freeway, over snow fields,
past frozen trees that lean and hiss.
It's hard-to-breathe weather.

Propped against the overpass wall
a pink ten-speed leans, the chrome spokes
and cranks caked with slush,
the pedals squeaking in the wind.
The near footprints fill with tiny drifts.

Behind one pair of headlights
approaching from a mile away, a man
swipes his windshield with a fast-food
napkin, streaking it with grease.
Ash from his bent cigarette
drops onto the spread map on the dash.

Staring into the frenzied glitter of flakes
in the headlight beams, his wife
places her hand on her pregnant belly.
Due soon, just beneath the thin curve
of flesh, someone new kicks and shifts.

Just then their car jolts with a deep thump
under the floorboard. Pulling off the road,
the man calms his wife, then climbs out
into the shock and blur to see what they hit.

I am buried in a dream
when he stands over me
in my bedroom hours later.
He puts his hand on my shoulder,
says my name until I open my eyes.
It's my brother. It's after midnight.
Come with me, he says, *I'll explain later.*

In the self-service car wash garage
ice hangs from the soap wands, pipes,
and drain gates. We unjam the coin slots;
hot soap gushes from the hose.
We take turns. As one sprays
the undercarriage, the other gags
and retches, bent over near the car.

Soap suds pink with blood, mixed
with thin bits of flesh, bone chips, and hair,
drip from the axles, wheel wells, muffler
and tires. With my glove I flick a shred
of muscle tissue from the shoulder
of my brother's winter jacket.

Under fluorescent lights, we are pale
and terrified. Our gasps hover as mist
and disappear. Only a handful of hours
and miles behind us, someone pedals
a pink ten-speed bike into the wind.
She is sixteen years old and wears
a black prom dress, so from her perch
on the overpass she will fall with perfect grace.

It is all plotted out. As she wobbles
on the wall, her arms spread,
no one in her family knows
she's gone. The whole wide world goes on.
The moment she falls, a few miles
to the south, a man in a car opens
a map, spreads it across the dash,
lights a cigarette. *Almost there*,
he tells his wife, wiping his windshield.
Something in the trees opens, then, and lifts.

Skyline Angel

Many stories high, her nearly bare hourglass
figure tips toward the freeway's southbound
traffic. In a hint of bikini bigger than a pink
bedspread, holding a cigarette longer than the steeple
on the city's east side, she gasps—doused by spray
from a giant garden hose. Her promise—*more flavor,
less tar*—looms through haze and fumes
of this morning's standstill rush hour.
That's what I need: *more flavor* in my life, *less tar*.
I pray for her to lift me out of my car, King Kong style,
cradle me in the valleys and hills of her palm,
watch me with the twin moons of her eyes, as she snaps
her moorings, steps across the skyline into her favorite
blue pool, the Atlantic. But soon, *honk honk*, I'm back
in the exhaustive current of tar, rubber, hubcaps,
broken glass—the real world inch and squeak.
And soon, our angel delivers the truth again,
reveals her other side in the rearview: a rusted silhouette
of peeled paint and graffiti, facing the northbound
who leave the city. Either way, we watch her,
this figure bigger than life—looking for some new sign.
But daily the sign's the same, and the same
longing hangs from every face in this caravan:
the great lot of us lottery losers, clock-watchers,
secret dreamers waiting for our exit.

Death Revisited

Uber-exec in a silver Lexus, doused
with top-shelf cologne, hair slicked back
with inch-thick gel, cufflinks glinting,
pinstriped three-piece pressed, Death weaves
freeway lanes at rush hour, checks his cell,
taps an appointment onto his back-lit palm.
In an hour he's at work in his office
suite throne—glass desk and a panoramic view
of the metropolis. Cartoon of the archaic
reaper pinned on his door: a sick joke
from an underling gunning for his job.
The economy's slow. Health stores
and high-fiber diets of late
treadmill his early gains; he hasn't made
margin in months. But today he'll take
several thousand: 350 in a trans-Atlantic flight
in choppy altitudes. Tsunami in the Southern
Hemisphere, couple hundred in a car bomb,
Middle East. On his glass World Radar
tiny lights blink out. Toughest are the one-offs:
his black leather glove laid over mouths
of old women in nursing homes, pulled life-support
plugs, kids nudged into pools, dogs chased out
onto the street, gentle persuasion
in the suicidal's ear—*Just do it.*
But later tonight at a wedding, he kicks back,
leaves the workday behind, stirring
a double scotch as he watches two strangers dance—
a man with a heart condition ill-advisedly twirling

his partner. Midway through the ballad,
the man's knees buckle and down he goes
as the crowd opens and gasps, a dark peony
of bodies blooming under chandelier light.
Somewhere a siren starts its futile wail
as Death, our debonair, slips out
toward home and sleep.

Live Worms Found in Shuttle Debris
—AP News Headline, 5/1/03

Drawn upward from the safe earth,
flushed from their dark universe
of soil and spring grass, there would be
the wreckage of this exodus of worms
those May mornings, as we neighborhood
children tiptoed barefoot through
the spilled noodles strewn
on our glistening street.
Some sat half-flattened by cars, some
brittle, lay like scattered question marks.
Others pulsing fat, gooey and slow, tunneled
their soft bodies back toward home.
And there on the driveway an imprint,
a final sentence scrawled across the mud
for us to decipher, a vapor trail—
like the one burned into the blue
southwestern sky and across NASA's glass screens
by the shuttle Columbia as it failed to return
to Earth one recent February morning.
Today, months after this disaster, I see
the headline: *Live Worms Found in Shuttle Debris*,
and stare at photos of these only survivors,
C. Elegans, an ancient breed brought on board
as an experiment, their bodies small as pen tips.
I wonder what answer we'd hoped to unearth
by sending them into deep space, heaped
and squirming in petri dishes, only to dig
them up again here, yielding no clues.

One thing's sure: we'll continue upward
for as long as it takes, despite the flubbed
liftoffs, the disappearing radar blips,
despite the last recorded gasps
of the crew, our miners smothered
by the night sky; upward despite the chance
of more manned rockets bursting
like Roman Candles over Canaveral's sea
of breathless witnesses, upward until we scrape
the roof of this dark cave to find light,
upward until we swallow what we hunger for,
until we slip through this wormhole
to feed on the heart of God.

All Heaven's Hotline Switchboard Lights

blink with distress again tonight,
each like a glowing city ablaze
in a war-torn country below.
Exhausted angels, their ears ringing

from human complaints, twitch tired wings
consoling the strangers on the phone.
Each caller's voice crackles with grief,
mixed with a fever of bliss and awe

they've reached the highest place:
I need to speak to God please...
most begin to say, their words
trembling like a game-show contestant's

near the ethereal assistant.
This request, like calling the CEO to fix
their faulty axle, receives polite, angelic refusal.
Then let me talk to my parents...

urges one person. *Let me win the lottery—*
cries another, irate—*It's me, you know...
I preach The Good News on Channel 78.*
One man, shaken, sobbing, gets through

from a crowded train station phone on his first try:
Hello Heaven?... Is this the Prayer Hotline? Then screams—
I CAN'T LIVE WITHOUT HER ONE MORE NIGHT...
Seconds later, his body, crushed by the jealous mob

slumps to the floor, his hand
still clutching the phone. The crowd
gawks at the torn connection, at the wires
dangling from the blessed receiver.

The world's leading clergy clash
with scientists on every TV station.
They debate the meanings of, and/or verity of
the miracle and/or hoax. But those who got through

to heaven—they float through their lives
holding the treasure map of sweet truth.
And the unlucky—those tortured for days,
months, even *years*, by the teasing beep

of the busy signal—they flail and screech
like rattled birds, their fingers and toes
mangled from hitting again and again the same
numbered buttons. Behind iron bars on high

hospital windows, they scream until
their voices die. Then, covering their ears,
they hold their skulls like giant bells
that ring forever and signal nothing.

The Messiah Complex

Holy shit, I shouldn't be ashamed.
It would be impossible for anyone to return
to whatever Earth-shattering business
occupied them prior to this talk show.

This morning's opening guest is Jesus Christ,
a.k.a. Rodney Schlenker—an investment banker
who received news of his divinity (in a dream,
which fits) at age 13, and kept it a secret

for 20 years. Can you imagine the weight
of that secret? But here's the utter mess:
before the first commercial, this guy, who appears
your average Joe, convinces me he is it—the *one*,

you know, the Savior, the new and improved—
to the point that I'm feeling pretty damn Roman,
sitting here with my remote. Like, who am I
to know, you know? I mean, he knew

The Good Book front to back, in fact, he even
remembered some stuff he said back then.
Anyway, after the ads it starts getting goofy.
The second guest is also Jesus Christ, a.k.a. "Justin."

Well, he proves the first a fraud
by looks alone. He is totally the one:
toga, thong sandals, beard, long locks,
the whole shebang. Way more of a Jesus

than Willem DaFoe. And he knew his stuff, too.
This Jesus has known since childhood
and already has followers, though this
is his first TV appearance. The questions the host

asks these two are kind of irreverent, like:
"so why don't you stop war and famine?"
But their perfect answers, and the way
they respect one another makes me wonder

why there can't be two Jesuses? I really don't see
why not. But wait. Everything gets weird
with the third guest, who calls himself "Jehovah,"
and looks more like Charles Manson than anyone else.

This guy is a real wacko, says he found out
40 days ago by phone—what an obvious fake—
and starts cussing, calling the others "blasphemers,"
"hypocrites," and "****ing jerks." For a second,

it makes me think of when Jesus got pissed
in the temple, but no way is this guy
the one. Call me Doubting Thomas,
but Jesus wouldn't wear those glasses.

One Day I Will Rule the World

My wife tells me I said this last night,
a slack-jawed, dream-induced declaration
to her and the bedroom darkness

followed by a sinister giggle before falling
back to sleep. She laughed after I said it,
as she laughed this morning informing me

of my remark, though I listened intently,
beginning to conquer a small mountain
of dirty dishes in our kitchen sink. Sure,

I chuckled briefly too at the seemingly ridiculous
notion, the way I imagine Napoleon
or George W. Bush once must have,

the first time the gilded hilt
of a bloodstained sword
descended toward them through the clouds,

long before their vain campaigns.
But, let me tell you, this news is no
small burden, and floods the flaccid

heart of the simplest man. Looking back
over the shifting light of the landscape
of hours on this first day since learning

my destiny, I see how everything's
skirmish, then empire, as in the way
I bravely surveyed the world map

of my wrinkled palm this morning
seconds after I sliced it open
wiping the unsheathed bagel knife.

That scarlet lake of blood in the lumpy hills
of my dishpan hands:
I wanted to give it a name.

The Man Who Names Wars

We've come so far in the art—
from such early shots in the dark
as *The Revolutionary War* (with a far
from revolutionary name), *100 Years War* (oh, please),
World War I (to end all wars...until) *World War II*
(and counting...), *The Korean, Franco-Prussian,
Vietnam* (...insert new country) *War.*
In fact, only a couple decent stabs
on the whole bloody list: *The War of the Roses*
and maybe the *Civil War*, at least an oxymoron.
In his defense, whoever held this post then,
The Man Who Names Wars,
probably named these after the fact, or during,
while scalped and bleeding on horseback
or limb-less in a last haze of morphine,
not thinking the rest of us will need
to live with these names forever.

But now we know the act of naming wars
is half the battle, so we're pre-emptive
and precise, finding our target
audience long before the war begins.
Somewhere deep in the Pentagon tonight,
no doubt, a new think tank's burning midnight oil
as we speak: the top brass's army of creative hired guns,
those sloganeers who, given the scope
of a future mission, are cocking their pens—
aiming for a new name. We can only guess
where this platoon's been recruited from:

a few failed poets pulled from the rank and file,
an ex-Hallmark vet fond of Wilfred Owen,
and one who went AWOL mumbling Tennyson in '46.
Whoever they are, make no bones about it:
they know no one will buy it
if it doesn't taste just right. It's got to have pizzazz,
a fierce logo: spurned Uncle Sam emerging
from thunderheads, and a drum-roll name
that makes even the diehard doves go hawkish
when they see it on FOX. Just listen
to these recently labeled products roll in:

Desert Storm, Desert Shield,
Operation Enduring Freedom,
The War on Terror...
can't you feel your heart
go full-on Bald Eagle at these names?

It's clear there've been major advances
in this field; we've learned
you can't just call hot sauce: *Hot Sauce.*
Instead, try: *Sergeant Frank's Flamethrower,*
or *Jumpin' Jack's Ass-Kickin' Fire Juice...*
We've learned a well-named war
will scorch the tongue.
So in the end, rest assured,
there'll be no World War III,
but *Operation Global Infernal Glory...*
they're already dipping their quills for that one.

Making Sure the Tractor Works

A drunk man reels his tractor around
the square lawn, midnight. His wife stares
from the front door window as if
on a half-sunk ship's deck at a shark

tearing through dark water. She chews
her thumbnail raw. Two of their sons, in blue
pajamas, shuffle across the linoleum
rubbing their eyes. She plays the bear

again, gets them to giggle by growling,
by chasing them upstairs to bed. She tucks
them in, strokes their hair, the air thick
with model train glue, sneakers, and fear.

The tractor, roaring, rumbles under the window.
*Dad works very hard, boys. He's just
making sure the tractor works, now go to sleep.*
She blesses their foreheads, leaves the door

open a crack, and disappears. Down the hall
her voice leaks into the phone.
The older boy buries his head
under his pillow as his brother climbs in.

Dad's grinding orbit rattles close,
then off around the house. Rattles close,
then off around the house. His headlights
wobble onto their wall as he bounces over the lawn,

the driveway, the flowerbed, the sandbox.
Shadows of tree branches drag across
their trophies and team photos, down
their closet door and away. When sunlight

breaks their windowpane, they wake late
for school and dress with no words. The bus
thunders past their house. They stare at soggy stars
and moons floating in their cereal bowls.

Outside, in her nightgown, their mother
stumbles over the rutted lawn barefoot,
pressing clumps of sod back down.
She chucks into a bag the evidence,

in scattered pieces, of last night:
a shredded mitt, a mangled plastic bat,
a headless action hero. She backs the tractor
into the shed, then stashes the keys.

She stands upright: the birdbath, the statue
of Mary from the crushed rose bed—prays
to herself, and turns toward the house,
toward whatever else she can still repair.

Crooked Wisdom

Having learned last night of his wife's affair,
my dentist holds a giant silver spear
and leans over the canyon of my open jaw.
Diving in again, vulture-sure, he picks

at my gum's weak pink flesh. Between
cliffs, down in the bone and coral landscape
of my teeth, nerve tips burst and bloom
like crimson flowers on a hill. Soon

blood's smeared red signature runs
from a deep root and floods my tongue.
Half-under with gas and lovely numb,
I watch his left eye become a clouded moon,

then one black branch of an eyelash
catch a teardrop's sheer balloon. With quick
shame, like a lion tamer stricken with naked
fear, he leaves the work of the open mouth

and the raw wound to another. He lays
the mirror down beside the spear and exits
the room. Anesthesia doesn't dim his grief
a room away. I hear the hygienist say:

She's leaving you for him. You've seen this
coming for a year...

A bit later he returns, composed in his white
smock, and clips the X-rays of my teeth
to the board. Then he lifts his pointer
to the slideshow of my bite: backlit, exposed,

the skull's little ornaments hang; bicuspids
and molars glow with hunger and decay. *See here—*
he points—*here's the abscess. Here's the cavity,
and here's that crooked wisdom pushing through.*

Heimlich in Candlelight

You leap from your chair, shock-white, mute,
as if stricken with the ultimate truth.

The other guests set down their forks,
bemused by your look of stunned revelation,

your wide-eyed awe. But the woman who knows
your secret—*thank God*—quickly backs you up:

her doubled fists thrusting your sternum.
A half-chewed chunk of stew, launched

with your furball guttural, lunges
across the table like a sick black moth.

Like silent monks who can't take it anymore,
some guests burst into an uproar of chortles,

as you gulp the air, newborn. Candle-thrown
and awful, your shadow swallows the wall.

Boy with a Trumpet in a Burning House

The only sounds sadder than the madhouse
wails of the Fox Hills fourth grade
orchestra rehearsal that autumn
were the solo screeches and moans

emanating from my bedroom
as I stood practicing, my trumpet
aimed like a loaded musket
at the closed door. Bleating octaves

the shade of slaughtered sheep's
blood sputtered and sprayed
from that flared brass bell as I bent
ancient harmonious scales

into twisted black sculptures of air.
A mouthpiece for ugly music,
with one tortured note I could blow
out the smoke creeping under my door—

that cigarette smoke that rose
from the kitchen, where my parents
slid skewers into the tender meat
of each other's hearts, neatly

paring their marriage to the bone.
It was murder learning those songs,
staring at bar graph notes
fading like a line of black birds

on telephone wires in fog. Lifting my
instrument, *chin up*, as instructed,
I didn't notice its pistons and valves
flecked already with a reflection

of the far wall's curtain of flame.
Fingers smudged with ash, a burning
in my throat, I'd turn the songbook's
yellowed, curling pages, close my eyes

to play the song no one could bear.
Twenty years later, standing outside
that house in my memory, I hear
the same old tune. There's the brass flare,

the burning song. There: the smoke-filled
hallways, the kitchen's shattered glass.
There: my sisters and brothers passing
soot-stained windows, turning a TV's

melting knob, humming as they watch
from the couch just catching fire.
No one in the house will see these flames
until fifteen years later and somehow

we'll all get out alive. Standing here now
in the clear air, looking in, I don't know
whether to tell the boy to play louder
or to let this song just burn and burn.

SHEPHERDS AND ANGELS

In a gymnasium's makeshift theater
the third grade takes the stage.
Down in the audience of wide smiles,
of flashbulbs, suits, and fur-coats—
I am disheveled, I am smoke,
I am the family on the yard watching their house burn,
the chairs around me empty.
Up there, third row, second from the left,
my nephew, a shepherd, hoists a large
cardboard candy cane, squinting through lights
to look for his family. He doesn't know yet
about this morning's fire: his molten plastic toys,
the TV a lump of melted black and glass,
nails driven backward through the standing walls,
a charred shingle simmering on the frosted lawn.
His class, in off-key dreamy voices, sings:
Christmas is Jesus' Birthday, Birthday...
This day Our Savior reigns...
Their fingers point to heaven, to the iron ceiling
where a wire-hung tin foil star sways,
sparking crinkled shards of broken silver light.
Why do we do this to our kids?
The world with its drunks and accidents,
its dropped cigarettes, the flames licking
the windows over this stage—
and our little ones, year after year, kneeling
under yellow crayoned haloes, placing
the paper crown on the plastic baby's head.

Still Shot

—for Gerald A. Fanning

Someday, I might remember you Dad,
with a black video camera plastered
where your head should be, viewing me
half-lit through the long glass hallway
of a lens. You captured each of us

this way, your kids, your unwilling stars:
holiday dinners, barbecues, birthdays—
no event was too small to charge
the battery and get it all on tape.
How you loved covering these moments:

zooming in for a close-up shot
as you interview one of us on a new bike,
Christmas morning. Passing landscape shot
of one of our Little League teams taking
the field, trembling close-up of me

in the school play. You half watched us
grow up inside the TV, rewinding parts
you liked best, fast-forwarding over
all the static and dead airtime, re-living
these moments, late into the night

as you drank and we slept.
Sometimes I picture you
sitting there in the smoke-filled basement,

drunk unknown director, 3 a.m.,
squinting through a film of tears, watching

this life passing before your eyes,
wishing you didn't have to see it all
so far away. Those videotapes—your black boxes,
your plastic time capsules, rarely held
your image, as I remember: only your laugh,

your voice, your hacking cough.
You haunted every episode.
But all this gathered evidence
mattered little to the jury of flames
the day the basement caught fire:

the tapes melting, tightly wound reels
sizzling like fistfuls of hair. Memory's a bad camera
that only shows grainy, off-centered shots
of faces once they're gone.
I remember trying to remember

your face after the fire, after you left.
I'd lay staring into the dark of my room,
hoping in vain your image would develop.
Two years later you walked into a dimly-lit
church, visiting home in a cameo role

for your mother's funeral. Your gray face
barely visible in the distance between us,
you shuffled to an empty side pew, turned on
your new camera, and began to record
one of the saddest days of your life.

I had my eye on you the whole time,
picturing how this movie would look
when you played it back: close-up
of the coffin, of your sisters and brothers
sobbing, landscape shot of Father

giving a farewell prayer.
I focused on you,
beloved narrator, absent star—the one
who half misses the world we live in
so it won't be forgotten by us.

Scarecrow Cross

Scarecrow, what now? Once in a long
gone time, I stitched you thread by thread,
helped weave, across your wooden spine—
small thrush busy at a nest—a thatched cross
of arms, a tattered fashion of rags and rope

stolen from my father's chest. Now, the last stalks
sway and shiver as I watch you wrecked from far away:
in low approach, the crows arrive; the seed thieves
dive and dive. The murder's here. What now?
Two crows perch, one on each shoulder,

their talons here to unravel you. A dark caw,
a shred of feathers, one pecks the straw heart,
another claws the burlap face apart.
Should I pray? Should I turn away? Half stand
in hungry shadows, half fly in famished light.

Morning Glory

—for Nancy Carothers

One vine twist of belief left, in one night's
work of growth and twine—our porch railing
climber leans, green-veined, gleaming

upward for the astral sea. Tight-swaddled buds,
bulbous and dew silk, hold in each a glance
of silver moon and seed. Within every

potent womb, a blue blood-ready prayer
begins its push to bloom in morning light,
and with a furtive nightward eye, unfurl.

Who needs day? Before the sleepers lift
a lid, they've done deep work of birth
and song. In the short-lived petal flare,

the first flash, their violet blush reveals
a world the day won't show. Soon,
curling toward night again, they take

the quick and hollow glare—they bury
inward what they know, and hide before
the blaze ensues to burn away the dream.

The Discovery of Fire

Already deeply shunned, the strange caveman
(club-thumped a dozen more times
by the rest of the grunters
on yet another day's failed hunt)
snuck off to his rock bed
far from the cold dark cave
and began again his feverish
ritual under the glinting sky:
rubbing two sticks together
in sheer desperation, sharpening

his gasps and screeches into that first
fire-flaked note of wrought air, from a deep
glowing furnace where this friction
of passion and anguish fashions
these spit sparks into a *word*,
his heart's new torch against all darkness
which he brings, cupping his hands
and blowing it into the sky, to the rest—
this new tool bright enough,
this new weapon sharp enough
to build or destroy the world.

Watching the Wind Read

Walking back across the grass, I catch you
lying on my blanket, ruffling pages
of my journal, then howling as you nibble
each quotidian crumb. I should howl
back, point at your transparent thievery
the way a cranky weathervane
shows, with its steel finger,
the world your shifting ways.
But I pause behind a tree and spy.
I notice you don't linger
on any of my recent poems
which concerns me,
and I don't understand *at all*
why you bother to skip
to the empty pages at the end,
as if you think I wrote something about you
in invisible ink. And you spend *way* too much time
staring at those back-to-back pages
where I scrawled left-handed the line:
"I've given God to the birds" dozens of times.
I hope you know that's a line I'd never use;
and anyway, remember: this is none
of your damn business. Spare me
your breezy analyses, your easy erosion.
You're the guilty one here—
you snoop, you busybody.
But I have to admit, the longer I stand here
watching you stop at certain pages
as if you're examining a ransom note,

I feel released, lifted, *free*.
So, when my cover softly falls
I won't follow your flight into the trees.
I'll wait until nightfall to hear you whisper
the history of the world, the dead leaves
dropping one by one to lie
like small red facts, as you spread all our news
in your dialect of currents and hurricanes.

The Perfect Poem

Mostly bucktoothed loners in pickups
on the other side of midnight, New Mexico,
have seen it, the perfect poem.
Whirling disk, ever elusive, supersonic
immeasurable blip, God's glow-in-the-dark yo-yo,
it hovers, instantly epic and skywide
over the desert, moans a low deafening hum
loud enough to shatter distant windows, then gone.
One man, his bathroom flooded with a burst
of light, nearly cut himself shaving.
One woman reported she felt as if the top
of her head had been shorn completely off.
Missing person reports are on the rise.
Children, drawn to its celestial effulgence,
leave the screen door ajar, drop their teddy bears
on the dewy lawn. Some of the briefly abducted,
babbling to therapists, faintly recall—
its inhabitants, their questions, their probing.
Others their wide almond eyes.
It threatens the Government, who some say
have it trapped and dissected in a subterranean hangar.
I can't believe we're out here again tonight,
you and I, in the middle of nowhere, craning
our necks, sifting our galaxy's fool's gold,
hoping we'll find it or it might find us.
What if it *does* descend tonight, finally,
this interstellar cathedral, this floating city?
What should we do? How will we answer
if the jaws of its giant door open,
if its blinding mouth calls us out of this world?

Digital Intimates

Beneath us, over us, toward us—a web
of luminous threads—the network reels
its far spun luster. Through this optic channel
into us, our bits and secret data burn
through hair-thin glass and air. We, invisible—
watch the urgent cursor pulse, and grow
closer than touch or speech. Alone together
again tonight, your voice of misspellings
and broken clauses blinks and glides
single character by single character
across the dark face of my window. The glass
screen and 15,000 miles of mountain and ocean
can't divide us. Tonight, my satellite,
boot up, log on, give me long, slow
sentences. Lean out your window, describe
your present world. Decipher every bright thing
across the immediate sky, over the currents
and moonlit contours of your country.
Whoever you are, my disembodied anonymous,
my shared user, my instant linguist—imagine me
as you wish. Draw me through this interface
once more. Hold me close in this data stream,
until we dream our circuits dim.

Last Dancers

Windworn sparrows, the final hour's
dancers drop from flight and leave. Over tossed
confetti, balloons, and curls of ribbon, the last
couple sways, draped like late fall flowers.
Whirls and dips now slow, early grace flown,
they turn like moons of a planet spun astray.
The needle drags dust through vinyl grooves, playing
a grave and love-torn voice. Gravity wants all dancers down,
wants them fallen like the rest, whose once shined shoes
line walls in closets shut for years beneath their long
forgotten suits and gowns. A boxed red corsage, a song
lingers in them, as in a distant room, and they refuse
to listen. But last dancers endure, who year into year
lean into fading notes to keep the music near.

The Pioneers

A white saucer stubbed with ashes, the moon
laves with milky light the cacti and gravel
of Vista Avenue. Here, at *the peak*, young
lovers take advantage of the privacy and view.

In an azure Impala, a couple mounts and humps.
Muffled in this musk of sweat and vinyl,
they thrust and gasp. Done, they peel apart.
Great loves like ours are rare as desert ice,

says the guy, gazing through the windshield steam
at constellations they've given pop star names.
Kurt, Elvis, Janice, etc., shimmer above
as the girl, taking a drag, searches for a station.

The world is ours, she wails, whooping
out the window as he guns it and peels out,
leaving a trail of smoke and burning rubber.
Blaring riffs from power speakers carve

a chainsaw song into mountain curves
they rocket past. Sticking out its wrinkled head
from loose and layered folds of flesh,
a dusty lizard blinks, then darts across

the space the lover's car just left. Thwapping
bugs with its gummy tongue, it pauses
at a tossed condom. Hungry, it hopes to find
what lives or hides in this shriveled sticky cave.

All the Mind's Animals

graceful and apple-brained, search for their place
in the nightfall fields. One turns in dirt,
one blinks on a high branch, one lies serene
in windblown grass. Black-eyed and alert,

a flock chews the hillside bare. Over them,
far from home, the sole watcher glides who eyes
the slightest stirring in the grass: the pulse of prey
that digs to hide, luring the enemy down.

Hunters know: fear flushes the frenzied flight
of game into the clear; fear's the bleeding scent
that feeds the flesh. In the mind the scene's
the same: doubt, sensing dinner a mile off, snarls,

twitches its nostrils, cocks an ear. Leaving the den,
feeding hour, it tracks across the fields, headed for
the barn's dark. First gust of a storm front,
doubt shoulders the rickety door. Hungry,

it sweats to lick and crush the nested eggs.
Thrashing the rafters and windows, the winged one
wants out. All the mind's animals, deep as the farmer
sleeps, scratch at low fences, threatening to leap.

Jellyfish

Gorgeous horror, saintly in your sheer gown,
you lift and swell, hovering here
and there, a hellishly elegant ascension.
Each clear pulse pushes you higher.

One slow spin closer, you slip translucent
in the current, now twirl a rippled fringe,
Medusa in a glance of surface light, loose
threads dangling as you lift, rouge-tinged,

reaching the crest. Now all our nerve tips,
mine and yours, so near this sweet burn,
flush with alarm. Tocsins ring as you dip
imminent, into trough, pink-fringed, and turn

your dance, your kiss of death, to the brink.
My flesh bristles at our potential touch.
Instant miss of sting and lash, you sink
blue-green, down, and leave no trace or stitch.

My Old Flame

A cluster of flushed foliage, rain-doused, this
maple remains lit from within, filled with an inferno
the finches and thrushes build. Leaping from branch
to branch, they arrange a morning symphony
flame by flame. The first bird's trill started this:
a mere flint spark flicked against the dry spine,
then every separate note ignites the wooden cage
like breath. Soon the whole tree glows like a Baroque
hall—a full ensemble tuning for an audience of one.

At the foot of this burning tree, like a pile
of wet black ash, a crow crawls onto the gnarled
toe-knuckle of a root. With her smoker's throat,
mad at sunrise, she calls out for another from across
the empty benches where I watch. Gorgeous torch singer
past her prime, widow with an awful cough,
she doesn't care if anyone hears her song.
Half dust already, lost in the chorus,
she flicks each spent match onto the grass.

IV

The Cloth Wings of the Woman

This morning, she leads you through
the carnival rides to a tent, its canvas
flaps roped taut to the packed straw
floor. *Welcome*, says the dwarf at the door

who takes your hand. *Leave your mother
your blue balloon*. Once inside, a dragon,
a monkey with a drum. Red wet frown,
the clown leans close. Here, you watch

and learn the dance: the elephant in a tutu,
the laughing giant, his swirling tattoos.
The dodge of knives, the quick whip
that snaps back the roar, tight calves

of the man who stands on the galloping horse.
The crooked gypsy finger, the flame swallower,
the wild-eyed dwarf, the tightrope wobble.
The ache and creak of the trapeze,

the cloth wings of the woman who falls
from the high swing like a moth, caught
in the net below. Then, the finale, the sudden
flood of light, the shadowed façade,

sweat erasing the clown's face as he waves
goodbye, as the circus of a lifetime
draws to a close. Opening the tent flap
to dusk: thick fog and mist, the carnival's

once whirlwind show now long gone.
In the littered field, hunched beneath
a bent elm, the old woman turns.
In her hands, a wilted blue balloon.

Seaside Carnival, Late in the World

Before the boardwalk's backdrop
of black ocean, the apocalypse prophets
stand like a seawall, a row of solemn
nightfall gulls guarding what the waves
won't tell. In sneakers, baseball caps
and Dad's Club jackets, they hold for hours

their signs, hand-scrawled in permanent
marker, that warn of the Seven Seals,
the coming end. Over these doomsday
preachers, amusement park lights
reel and flash through blown sea mist.
In the salt sticky air, tourists pass

the stern believers, their faces lost
in cotton candy clouds. The cackle
of fun-crazed kids breaks the carousel bell
clatter; stretched into awful shapes, they shrink
in the hall of mirrors. A stroller's bent wheel
spins, rumbling across the boardwalk planks;

the pink baby rattle drops, and rolling, stops
at the black boots of one of the stone-faced
prophets. Gaps between the wooden slats show
the tide's incessant crush below. From somewhere
out in the dark water, a far red blink,
low foghorn moans over vast folds of ocean

and the clank of an anchor or buoy. Offshore,
like a fallen constellation, searchlights scan
the sandbar and shallows for three kids
pulled by waves from the jetty at sunset, hours ago.
On the beach, their mother clutches a deflated toy,
all that's been recovered so far. One by one,

the boardwalk lights go out. Tanned cashiers
tally the day's taffy and rock salt sales.
The silent prophets, with no measure of whom
they've sold on their notions, pack up their wares
until tomorrow. Soon, the slow bloom of stars
begins over the bleached, sand-beaten town;

the red hum of VACANCY blinks at the Oceanview
Hotel. Sunburned sleepers coil in cool sheets, as children
with flashlights sift through clams and conch shells,
their sandy treasures. Down at the dark shore,
all night long, the ocean keeps on doing
what it does—never knowing when it's done.

Old Bright Wheel

Listen to this chain grind,
this cranking wheel of light.
Listen to its slow fall
and rise, its turn and turn and turn.
How simply we could be stuck

here on top, or bottom;
this is an old ride, a senior citizen
of slow delight. Seems devoid, almost,
of passion, of that skyrocket surge,
that vehement near-death plunge.

But listen, this is the bright ride
I'm on, my revolution. What vast
distance from here, Ocean City
Ferris wheel. I cover one eye,
and miles away the frantic lights

of oceanfront casinos blur.
You see, I love her hand in mine,
our dismay, our trepidation.
I love this lock bar, this engagement
to the plastic seat, the family ride.

I love—*way down there*—
the prams and strollers,
the upward eyes. I love our doubt
about this slow pleasure, this turmoil,
this grind—even *more* after the greasy

ticket-taker's wisecracks about the age
and recent failures of this ride.
I love our secret urge to leap
at any lurch, any quick stop.
I love wondering if, up here, we might die.

The Roller Coaster

A humped and jagged junkyard site,
it drips moonlight—this mountain
of snapped planks and torn metal tracks.
Half of a crusted chain, its giant links
wrenched apart, hangs like intestines
draping the charred entrance sign.
Once called *The Spirit of Flight*—
the green paint of its cars graced
with bald eagles and biplanes—
now it lies, a pile of scrapped pipes,
peeling in the acid breeze
of a nearby factory, whose hissing
smokestacks billow a yellow gray dust.
Time must fell every thrill and structure.
A mangled rattle of rust and fracture,
razed beside an oil-slicked river
whose caked face sludges with trash and dross,
the whole heap creaks, then groans
as a gust shakes its buckled frame.
The skeletal rails erode
like the shell of a creature collapsed.
Its disconnected cars, that once
carried terrified and wide-eyed riders,
lay scattered like a cracked
spine through empty lots of shattered
metal bones: motors, TV's, fridges,
steel beams of road bridges, billboards,
hubcaps, bulldozers, blackened iron
husks of truck chassis, shopping carts,

tires, chunks of pavement.
What will remain when this world ends?
When the top wobbles and turns on its rim,
tossing clock cogs, sprockets, coils, spokes, cranks, bolts—
the blueprints dust and all the palaces ash.
Beaten engine, every screen blank,
the whole globe's axis bent.
Imagine that night. Blackout, each of us lost
in our huddled ruins, scared of the wind.

Picturing the Lost World

America, here's your Roman cathedral,
your stately ruins, this ancient,
chipped-paint drive-in. Echoes live on
in this deco graveyard: gurgle of a slurped
shake, bouncing shock-squeak

of a parked, shark-finned Thunderbird,
windows fogged. Scent of pink lipstick,
french fries, hair grease, burger with cheese.
Red cursive buzz of a tall neon sign
—*Star Drive-In*—knocked and stained

by moths. The glow and flit of cigarette tips
and fireflies, rockabilly reverb from the dead
diner jukebox. Fist fight back of the lot
broken up by cops. In trees, the swaggering
shadows of teens flirt in headlight beams.

And up there, look, three stories high
on the altar's cracked cement screen—looming
over this dream of congregated hotrods,
the ghost of our goddess screams, as our god,
arrow-struck, aches to reach his rifle in the dust.

Happiness

Happiness, that fatted calf, hangs
from the ceiling by a thread. Silly-eyed
and frilly, the piñata teases, swaying
like a plump ballerina above the birthday
party guests. When the blindfold goes on,
when laughter and light disappear,

I'm told to thrash the high darkness
until I hit it. Look at me: the village idiot
shaking my fist at the night sky, taking
jabs at its flank, hoping to stab the elusive
cloud, to start a shimmering candy river
for all the thirsty villagers below.

I know they watch from behind the windows
of their dark homes, dreaming the red gold rain.
We each want a taste of it, thirst for it, want it
to fall in our hair, to bounce from our palms,
to get on our knees and thrust our fists
into its shattered rainbow shards.

We won't stop until the last sun-flaked drop
spills, until every piece of joy's flash flood
is gone. And when it's done, when we're all
singing over short candles, slurping bloodred juice
from our thumbs, playing with our new toys—
after the lucky kid fishes one last piece

from the sea of wrappers, we'll be sure
not to look *up*—where that gutted cardboard carcass
arcs like a hung God, dragging like a sharp
pendulum over our heads, a drained slab on a hook,
a reminder of the dry season, of need and loss
and the empty hours we've all long forgotten.

The Slide King

One year older with each step
up the steep ladder, you finally reach
the slide's top platform, as your sons
and daughters laugh and splash, treading
water below. Out in the middle of the lake

the slide wobbles, its rusted flanges squeaking
on a soggy, splintered raft. Looking down
from under your tilted crown of storm clouds,
you faintly smile—white-knuckling the steel railing.
Draped on the legs and slick steps, black-green

weeds hang like snakes. Passing you, one after
another, fearless kids plunge headlong down
but you don't move. When we climb the steps
to stand beside you, you shiver, pretending
you enjoy a crow's nest view. For the first time ever,

at this height, the fathomable depth of you—
by a quiver, by this real and visible fear
is revealed. So you inch to the edge
like a blindfolded sailor on the plank, and take
the quick slide with strange, unexpected glee,

down into your drinking cave. Taken
by the lake, you sank into the muddled wake
like a silver medal of an unknown saint, stolen
from my neck by a wave. Years pass before
a wash of tumbling autumn silt deposits you

on land again, sober, so many years younger
but many years old. Standing, you rub
your eyes, escaping your deep sleep to see:
the slide long gone, your sons and daughters grown,
on the shore upended boat hulls drying in the sun.

The List of Good Names

Tonight, in the family style
pizzeria, we speak of having a child
some day. On a napkin smudged red
where the leaky felt tip lingered,
I watch meteors, sperm and tadpoles
cross the paper sky, as you
draw up a list of good names.

Looking at the list, I'm a substitute
teacher practicing attendance
before the class arrives:
Isabella, Gabriel, Rose. Who will be
the bookworm, the athlete, the clown?

Around us, the families finish
dinner, pack into minivans and leave.
The pimpled waiter picks up
broken crayons, wipes sauce
from a plastic high chair,
unplugs the video game.

Soon the room's as silent
as a doll shop after hours.
When I'm ready to speak, above
the ticking of the clock, my rubber
lips click. Whispering the list's
first name, I hear the voice

I used when I spoke your name
the first time—that voice I've used
when I try the name of an unknown
plant, or when I'm scared, or when
I pray, or when I know a stranger
now listens in the next booth,
the one I thought was vacant.

Tributary

Miles away, Aunt Joyce drifts
in the slow flood of her dying,
lying in the cancerous raft
of her body. Here in this house,

we wait in separate rooms for news
of her imminent death, avoiding
the telephone, that black tumor
on the wall, its dark cord a dangling hook.

Every hour's a floating mountain
of ice grinding past the window.
Late in the day, when the wave
of her death crashes into us, we're drawn

into the living room. Sitting with
the mourners, Aunt Joyce's shattered
family, each clinging to each other,
I cradle Gabriel, my infant son.

Watching his face, I see
a sudden great smile surface—
a bright fish, a sweet foolish leaping.
Almost ashamed, I move to cover it,

this untimely delight on the mouth of my son,
all stirring and giddy, who has yet to learn
the appropriate response to death
or who is only just trying to teach us.

V

Green Stephania

A full wood, wet bark
shower, the fresh drenched
trees, the leaves lush heavy,
so consequently, Stephania.

Stephania, curled finger ferns
unfurl and burst. Loose spores
string through mist and nestle.
Moss tufts rub.
Rain-slapped leaves, Stephania,
spring and drip on our deep
sogged glade, our soaked sunk roots.

Me and Stephania.
In a hiding place our slick lips sore
from pressing together.
Stephania, seaweed breath,
burrs in your tangling curls,
soiled nails and knees, giggling.
Eden, Stephania. The smell of dirt.
I never want to leave the world.

Through the streaming wash
of rain, through the windows
and pale curtains, our mothers ache.
Their bedrooms flicker with blue TV.
Scent of biscuits, chimney smoke, tea.
Our fathers cup their hands

against the cold glass panes
and look out.

It's dusk, Stephania.
No one knows where we are.

Pedinkis

Not, as one might think, a Greek god
or a cloaked and lonely monk,
shrunk beneath his hood on a cliff's edge
in the rain. Not a game the old folks

might play, on peeling card tables in some
musty hall. Not even the grand Roman
nomenclature of some bulbous affliction.
Well, close. It's what my mother called the thing

beneath the fleet of red toy boats bobbing
through the apple-scented bubbles in the bath,
giving me the sponge. *Wash your pedinkis...*
she'd say. That pink word slithered toward me

through the steam, as she pulled the drain
and turned her head toward the door.
Eyeing the intricate patterned swirls of her
curls and bobby pins, I'd reach in elbow-deep

as if to slay some eel, or worse, worm—
this thing she couldn't touch or even see.
Finished, I'd say, looking down at my toys
bunched in the whirlpool over the drain.

John's Knees

Here comes my older brother John,
tough pudge of a kid, slouching down
St. George's School steps.
Shirt untucked, loose-tied, capless,
he roughs into the boy crowd of blunt
punches, thumps another kid, gets laughs.

Diving into the station wagon back seat
he pile drives me, whacks my cap off,
yanks my tight tie tighter, slugs
my bony thigh full-fisted. He is my *big*
brother. I am sore ribs and a stomach ache
under a British History book.

A pale acolyte blessed by his knuckles,
twig-kneed and jealous, I peek at his legs
as he falls asleep halfway home.
Thick as tree stumps, his hairy thighs bulge.
But his *knees*, those flesh lumps with scabbed

escutcheons. Blood chunked with black
and purple armor, his knees like plump
raspberries caked with mud and sweat.
Let me run down Death Hill with you,
I should tell him.
Show me how to bleed.

Sissy

Under a right field fly ball's rare arc
stands the one who throws like a girl.
On the bench, the team rises like a jury,
their jaws dropping. The coach's dusty
heroes, the infielders hang their heads,
afraid to watch. Beneath the falling orb,
the ball that holds the whole game's fate,
the right fielder stares into the sweet deep
cavern of his mitt. There, a trapped monarch
flutters in the leather web, the wings
paper-graceful, the legs puppet threads.

Killer Raccoons at Sleeping Bear Dunes

"Perpetual peace is a futile dream."
  —Gen. George Patton

After proposing to my girlfriend at sunset
on the beach at Sleeping Bear Dunes,
we strolled, two happy campers, up the dark trails
toward our tent at the edge of the woods.
By primeval instinct, already sensing my new role
as hunter and protector, I clutched her hand—
the hand of my *fiancé*—to show her that nothing,
no saber tooth, no tribal warrior, no witch
or bogeyman would ever harm her now.
Reaching our cave-like campsite, I hunted
in our Dodge Shadow for the fire-starter kit
while she set the table and started to cook.

Half a bottle of lighter fluid later,
after torching the entire Home and Garden
section of the newspaper, I had that twig pile
blazing. Toasting to our future, we clinked
our wine glasses and began our feast. Moments later,
disturbed by a rustle in the brush, I shined
my industrial, wide-beam flashlight into the woods,
revealing, *right there*, the whites of enemy eyes.
Crouched, ready to attack, were a hundred
or at least a dozen raccoons. Every soldier,
old or new, knows when to defend a stronghold
and when to retreat. So, turning from them,

we grabbed what we could, then dashed
fast as antelopes, our hearts pounding with primal
horror, into the Shadow and shut the door.
And out they crept, this platoon of bloodthirsty
raccoons, to plunder our rustic love nest. Fearless
and furry, these furious murderers, these long-fanged
night demons devoured our dinner as we watched
from our car. Whispering *the bastards
won't come near our wine*, I passed the bottle
to my wife-to-be for a swig. Already, I could see
that she loved my soldier swagger, my urge to prey,
my potential for glory in the terrible wild.

Gullsong August

A hushed drove of gulls gathers
on the shoreline, dusk. A beak's
occasional cluck, a ruffle of ashen feathers.
Causing flutters and squawks, you sneak

toward this solemn conference, your feet
bare in cooling sand. An army of gray
watchers, flustered by your advance, they retreat
with every inch you move their way.

When at last you burst into them—a rush
of laughter, your arms splayed like wings—
what a symphony you start, a flourish
of soaring notes, your hands conducting

a whirlwind of birds, a shrill flash of song
and flight—circling over us, over the whole beach,
the ocean; some gulls glide low along
the shore, some dive high, others screech

and tumble in wild orbits—every bit
of this chaos in me because of you:
this flush and flurry, this rise, this fit
of grace inside, this plunging through.

For My Wife, Who Sleeps

This late, you've gone to depths
beside me, our bed a tipped raft
in a dark sea. Sinking fish,
you twitched twice
before leaving me here

in our once shared element of air.
Your body parts the sheet and turns,
your hair like a scarf left floating
in a wake, a mere surface clue
to where you truly are.

Where *are* you now, lost swimmer,
in what chasm, what womb? What blue
pulls through your gills, beneath
the near morning's baited lines of light?
Why can't I follow you into this dream?

I'd never want to outlive you,
to be cast off like one of those lost sailor's
wives, left to stare into a deep sea-grave
of sleep. Can you hear them now,
wherever you are, these widows' cries

screeching like whale songs,
a trailing dirge of un-tuned violins?
They're cursed with life alone.
Nightly, low tide, they walk
the weed-strewn pier for hours,

watching frayed ropes
whip abandoned docks.
Scouring like gulls the shoreline debris,
they tear bare knees on shells
and beach glass, digging

for some piece—a scrap
of sail, mast-shard, anchor fluke,
rib, flank, bone, hull, compass—
whatever points the way
to what the waves report as lost.

Song of the Sea to the Shore

Unraveling velvet, wave after wave, driven
by wind, unwinding by storm, by gravity, thrown—
heaving to reach you, to find you, I've striven
undulant, erosive, blown—

or lying flat as glass for your falling clear
down: I can't swallow you. So why
have I felt I've reached you—as two reflected stars,
surfaced, lie near—as if the sky's

close element is one in me, where starfish
cleave to stones—if you're so far?
I've touched you, I know, but my rush
subsides; our meetings only leave desire's

fleeting trace. Every place I touch you
changes shape. Shore, lie down—
undo. I'll fill your thirsty bones with blue.
I'll flood your every cave and we'll be one.

Song of the Shore to the Sea

It's never enough being one. Why do I hope
to contain you, always undoing and undone;
every place you touch me changes shape.
It's not my way to just lie down,

to sink, effaced and full. If you
swallow me, you're drained, and half
of us is gone. Desire's fulfillment is *two*,
not one, or our tidal meetings are through.

So hurl your wet force forward, sea,
take me wave by wave. Pearl maker, pull
me deep; our one's a need, a momentary
bliss. What I erect, you spill—

castles, boulders, cliffs. My love's endurance
grain by grain; your adoration's rain.
Touch my bones, my canyon's carved evidence.
Even the moon that moves you is stone.

Acknowledgments

The author wishes to thank the editors of the following publications, in whose pages some of the poems in this book first appeared.

America: "Gullsong August"
Barbaric Yawp: "The Roller Coaster"
Eye Dialect: "Green Stephania," "Failed Existentialist in a Field of Fireflies," "My Digital Intimate"
Inkwell Magazine: "Standing in the Shed Light"
Limestone: "Sissy"
Ploughshares: "Making Sure the Tractor Works"
Poetry: "The Song of the Sea to the Shore," "The Song of the Shore to the Sea"
The Cape Rock: "Last Dancers"
The Dry Creek Review: "John's Knees"
The Furnace: "The Discovery of Fire"
The Hawaii Review: "Interstate 75"
The Ledge: "Pedinkis," "All Heaven's Hotline Switchboard Lights"
The Listening Eye: "One and a Half Miles Away from Dying"

The title "All the Mind's Animals" is taken from "The Kingdom of Poetry" by Delmore Schwartz.

Special thanks to Peter Markus who reeled in this book and hammered it to a telephone pole; to Mariela Griffor and Marick Press, and to Tim McMahon, editor of The Ledge Press, who published *Old Bright Wheel*, in which some of these poems first appeared.

Great thanks to Tom Lux for his brilliant guidance, his friendship and support, to Marie Howe, Suzanne Gardinier, Kate Knapp Johnson and the Sarah Lawrence Writing Community. Thanks to my friends and poets in Detroit and at InsideOut Literary Arts Project, who've encouraged me in recent years, especially Terry Blackhawk, who brought me under her amazing wing. Thanks to David Peterson for his advice and support.

Special thanks to Mom for the words, Dad for the poetry, Mike and Mary Clare for your steadfast support—to my whole family —who shaped my heart, and to my wife and son, who own it.

Robert Fanning received a B.A. from the University of Michigan and an M.F.A from Sarah Lawrence College. His poems have appeared in *Poetry, Ploughshares, The Atlanta Review, The Hawaii Review, America, The Ledge, ArtWord Quarterly* and other journals. He is the recipient of a Creative Artist Grant from the Michigan Council for Arts and Cultural Affairs, the Foley Poetry Award and the Inkwell Poetry Award. His first book, *Old Bright Wheel*, won the Ledge Press Chapbook Award. He is the Program Director for InsideOut Literary Arts Project in Detroit.